What Worked for Me!

By Richard Bilesimo

Disclaimer

This publication is protected under the US Copyright Act of 1976 and all other applicable international, federal, state and local laws. All rights are reserved, including the right to reproduce this material or parts thereof in any form.

Please note that this publication is based on personal experience. Although the author has made every reasonable attempt to achieve complete accuracy of the content in this Guide, they assume no responsibility for errors or omissions. The author makes no guarantees in regards to results related to this Guide. The self-help contents are solely the opinion of the author and should not be considered as a form of therapy, and/or diagnosis or treatment of any kind: medical, spiritual, mental or other.

The purchaser or reader of this self-help Guide assumes responsibility for the use of these materials and information. You should use this information as you see fit, and at your own risk. Your particular situation may not be exactly suited to the examples illustrated here and you should adjust your use of the information and recommendations accordingly.

Any trademarks, service marks, product names are assumed to be the property of their respective owners, and are used only for reference. Nothing in this Guide is intended to replace common sense, legal, medical or other professional advice, and is only meant to inform the reader of what worked for the author.

Authors Comments

I was born in Tampa Florida where I lived until the age of thirty-six. For twenty-three years my world revolved around a life of drug use. At fifteen I tried crack cocaine for the first time and by nineteen had become a junkie. I abused many different drugs, but my drug of choice was crack cocaine. Racking up quite a rap sheet I spent the better portion of my life in and out of jail. My name became notorious with the local Tampa Police, where several officers still know my name to this day.

You will notice the word affliction in place of addiction throughout this guide. I believe that the word addiction or addict has become almost glamorized in today's society. Everyone is addicted to something or has some type of addiction. An affliction is a condition of great suffering and distress due to adversity in one's life and it is not glamorous.

You must understand that I am not a doctor or a scholarly man for that matter. My education comes first hand on the streets of Tampa where I attended the school of hard knocks. It was there that I acquired my knowledge, experience and degree to write this guide.

People can say they can help you, but unless they have lived the life, they can never walk the talk. I say to you, everyday I have to walk my talk.

I have incorporated what worked and didn't work for me as I struggled to beat my substance afflictions. This guide is designed so that you can read it over and over again until you are free from your afflictions. It will teach you how to escape any affliction you may have, not just crack cocaine. I continue to use this guide to keep my own mind focused and my soul free.

If you're tired of repeating the same mistakes, then try something different. This guide may not be conventional and even a bit controversial.

It is a totally different approach to drug treatment then what is currently used, but does incorporate many things I learned from the numerous meetings, counseling, and treatment centers that where part of my struggle to free my soul. This guide is what worked for me.

I pulled myself up from nothing to rise above the ashes to find freedom for my soul. I now dare you to accept my challenge. Buy this guide and I believe you too will beat your afflictions and become a winner.

ACKNOWLEDGMENTS

I would like to give a special thanks to the following people who have helped me, inspired me and encouraged me during my long struggle to over come all my past afflictions. Bethel Gillespie - My loving grandmother, who loved me unconditionally to the very end. Judith Estep - My loving mother who always gave her support and love as she endured the hell of having to watch her beloved son destroy his life. Judge Don C. Evans – For acknowledging me as a human being instead of just another junkie as I stood before him in court. Tampa Police Officers Gary Garboski and Jeff Wilks – For always trying to inspire me by talking to me about being a better person as well as that it was never to late to change my life. Patrick Curry – For always being there to pick up the pieces when I was at my lowest. John Roundtree – For helping me when I needed it the most. Paul Lunter - For giving me a second chance that lead to the road of my success. Tim Elliott - For taking a chance on me and teaching me many useful things that know one ever took the time to teach me. Yvonne and Linda from JTL who brought my wife and I together while supporting us. Silver Zagrodnik -My wife for believing in me before I believed in the possibility that I could change my life as well as standing by me through thick and thin. Alice Zagrodnik – For being a caring and understanding Mother-in-law. The Collette Family – For their encouragement and support during the final struggle of my battle for my soul. The Smith Family – For giving me the opportunity to learn the boat building trade, when most other companies would have denied me employment. Dave Kalinowski – For being an understanding work partner and friend. Garland Mason – For supporting me even after knowing my past. Mark Joiner – For accepting me as I am and being my friend. Willow – For spending countless hours listening to me and supporting my dreams. The many people, who tried to help me throughout my struggle that accepted me, did not take advantage of me and encouraged me to find my life.

CONTENTS

CONTENTS CONT'D

Introduction

Hello, I'd like to introduce myself. My name is Richard Bilesimo. I am a survivor of a twenty-three-year crack affliction and a sordid lifestyle. I am writing this guide for two reasons:

1. I would like to help those who are currently afflicted to know they can make it back from less than nothing.

2. So the loved ones of someone lost to drugs will know that there is always hope and never to give up on those they care about.

I am living proof that you can create a new life even if you have several severe afflictions in your life.

Before I decided to change my life, I lived in the same hell that you or someone you know may be trapped in now. I will admit it won't be easy, and you will have to do things you don't want to do. But the reward is freedom. If you have any or many afflictions, you must be ready and willing to change your life for this guide to help you. No one can force you to change. Change has to come from each and every individual. You may slip, and you may slip more than once. The key is to keep doing all that you can. Each time you recover and apply yourself once more, it will become easier and easier for you to follow the plan. If nothing else has worked before, and you are ready, I truly believe what I teach in this guide will make the difference in your life. You can escape from your self-induced hell. You just have to keep doing your best.

I am sure there will be things in this guide that you will not agree with, things you will not want to do and believe that you don't have to do. All I can say to you is that if you are reading this guide, then other things have not worked. So you have purchased this guide to make a difference in your life. So make the difference and follow what I tell you. Life is hard, but living life with the gorilla of afflictions on your back is even harder.

My prayers are with all of you struggling to take back your life. Know that you are not alone. There are people who care what happens to you. God bless you, and good luck.

The Term "Addiction"

"Addiction" to an abuser simply means "undoable." The term "addiction" only spawns disbelief in oneself. It is a negative term that creates nothing but negative results or insanity. Why? Because of what you tell yourself. If you say to yourself that you cannot get out of this dismal hell, then, guess what? It becomes reality. Because you are confirming it to yourself, it becomes a fact. It does not matter if it is unintended on your part. You are brainwashing yourself into believing you cannot change your life. Your lie becomes the truth because you believe that addiction is unbeatable. What you tell yourself has a great impact on what your future will be. You are living out your "addiction" because you believe you are an addict.

You are David against a giant named Goliath. David believed in himself and beat Goliath in the end. This is a fact from the Bible. Instead of using the term "addiction" use "affliction", "abuse", or "over-indulged habit". Habits can be broken, beaten, or overcome. What you tell yourself makes all the difference. The problems that you're struggling with seem doable now, don't they? Believe that you can overcome any obstacle in your life. You can take a negative belief and change it to a positive.

Understanding Affliction

What is an affliction? Afflictions are nothing more than habits that we overindulge to the point that we are out of control. You reach a point where this overfed habit consumes your whole being, creating a person totally out of control. Usually, other bad habits follow and add themselves to your first affliction.

Mine was crack cocaine, hustling, crystal meth, and the environment in which I chose to live. The other bad habits accumulate over time and feed the first bad habit of your choice. It leaves us so lost that we become totally confused and exist in the shadows of death itself. This is the wrong route altogether. You need to understand that this dismal hell you're living in started because of one wrong action due to an unidentified emotional reaction. The secrets you kept hidden from the rest of the world influenced your reactions. The unidentified emotions that you harbored are because you didn't have an understanding on how to deal with them. You had no understanding of how to handle your reaction to a particular emotion in the first place.

You may be angry, sad, embarrassed, depressed, peer-pressured, desperate, so forth and so on. In the beginning, if you had talked to someone, as I should have, then maybe our souls would not have ended up being trapped. That is why it is so important before you address your recovery to tell your secrets to someone whom you trust. Then you will begin to free the emotional reaction within your soul that caused all of this long ago. By telling all your secrets that until now you have not dealt with, you will help free the emotional reaction in your mind. Living your new positive life means life itself will take over your negative and gloomy past.

Why do we choose the path of affliction? During your affliction, you may experience many different negative emotions. You may be feeling alone, scared, or embarrassed or have a sense of worthlessness along with many other negative emotions. These emotions are closest to our hearts and souls.

All human beings are here on Planet Earth by one entrance: our mothers birth us. Suddenly, we are thrust into a world that forces us to find a routine and a balance in order to survive. What is balance? Balance is nothing more than a change that you'll have to introduce into your current life in order to fit into society. As children, we do not understand how important it is to find balance in life. Everything in life, good, bad, or indifferent, has balance. Even the earth itself has balance. That's how the world works.

After being born, we have two routes placed in front of us. One route sets us on the path of prosperity and righteousness, while the other route sends us down the path to destitution and evil. From infants to adolescents, we have very little understanding of how important our choices will be in our life. We have no insight or understanding of how the path we choose will affect our destiny.

We are born as nothing more than mimics. We mimic the people who inspire us, good, bad, or indifferent. For example, fathers, mothers, brothers, sisters, grandparents, friends, athletes, and so forth, will affect our choices. These people will teach or inspire us during our young years. If we are lucky, then those inspiring or teaching us are providing us with good, wholesome values and choices.

Our environment plays a big part of how we are taught or inspired. As an infant we can do nothing about the environment in which we are born. Many of us picked up bad habits from the wrong people in our environment. When we associate with the wrong people, we learn from them how to make bad choices, usually one right after the other. That is not to say that even those in a good environment don't make bad choices. You can grow up in a good environment and still meet people who make bad choices that will influence your choices. With that thought in mind I want you always to remember this:

"If you hang out with one loser,

you can never win."

What causes us to make bad choices? Hm…that's a good one. What is it that causes us to make a choice in the first place? Well, let's think about it. Most likely we have a reaction to an emotion that we don't understand. What causes this emotion in the first place? An emotion is created from any one of our senses as a triggered reaction. Seeing, hearing, smelling, touching, and tasting can cause negative and positive emotions.

An emotion is a spontaneous combustible pressure that's released all at once. It's like a volcano erupting. It releases pressure from deep within a place that is nearest your soul or core. This is the first place the emotions start. How much pressure is released from the core of the volcano determines the direction in which the lava will flow. It will either go up in the air or spill down the sides in one direction or the other.

Emotions cause a feeling and then a reaction to that particular feeling. The outcome is then an action. A volcano doesn't have as much power as a human being because the volcano cannot apply change of action. It is a victim of a building pressure. It cannot change the flow of the lava at will like a human can. As human beings we are different. We're given the power of choice itself. We alone have the last say over our actions. Again, emotions cause feelings, which in turn cause a reaction and then a choice. The reaction or choice will be either positive or negative. That depends on you.

Then you have the consequences or responsibilities for the action or choice you have taken. The current path, good or bad, you have taken, or had a reaction to, will determine your future path. If you make a bad choice, you will end up in misery, jail, drug rehabilitation, or exile. If you make a good choice, you get to move ahead and grow in your life. Remember, a choice can only be confirmed by your actions.

"Positive choices move you ahead in life."

If you have made a bad choice, you're probably not on the best terms with your parents, husband, or wife, especially if you have made the choice to smoke crack cocaine or do other drugs. You must remember that your family doesn't understand your emotions or why you react to them the way you do. Heck, you may not even understand why you react the way you do. People around you, as well as you yourself, may not know how to help you shake off this curse that controls you.

How Does One Escape?

What if I were to tell you that you yourself could break the curse in which your soul is trapped? Yes, you can free yourself from being trapped. You can set your soul free from your self-created hell. You just have to learn that balance is the key. An understanding of what these balances are is important. I'm going to share with you everything I know and learned during my struggle to escape my afflictions.

I was in hell, living a vicious cycle that took over my whole being for twenty-three years. I now have a newly created life along with the salvation of my soul. I was going down the wrong route because of my bad choices. My bad choices where influenced by my reactions to my emotions. I lived out my lessons the hard way and learned by them. It took a lot of trial and error to find a way out. With hard work and consistency I learned to understand my emotions. Graduating to this level isn't easy, but in the long run it is worth the effort. We are all worth the effort, and a positive life is definitely worth living.

The number of years you've been condemned to substance or other abuses will in great part determine how hard you have to work to change your life. You will need to learn how to control your reaction to the emotions that caused you to make the bad choices that led to your current imprisonment. You will have to learn to make good choices no matter how hard it may seem.

You can change and walk on the right route. The applications that I've created in this Guide are the ones that helped free my soul. The things I'm about to share with you are what I had to do myself in order to break free from my afflictions. I was constantly doing all I could to free my soul from the hell crack cocaine and crystal meth had created for me. I went to many different treatment programs during this time. Sometimes it was on my own accord and other times it was forced on me by the court system. Each time, I took mental notes of what worked and what did not work, formulating a formula for success. I spent seventeen years seriously doing all I could to free my soul from its cage. "Me, myself, and I" lived in a dismal hell that was my own soul's choosing.

The Applications

Application One: You will have to work on getting rid of the secrets that consume your mind and soul, good, bad, or indifferent. These would be the secrets that triggered the emotions that caused your bad reactions. There is only one way to do this. Pick someone of the cloth or someone you trust whole-heartedly with whom to share your secrets or emotions. The person you pick should also be the lead in your support team. Your lead support person needs to know everything about you in order to understand why you chose the path you did. Give the person you choose a copy of this guide so they will understand what you are going to do and what will be expected of them.

The people you choose for your support team should not judge you. These people you choose have to be winners. Remember, a winner is any John or Jane Doe that lives by society's standards. They should have good morals, values, and self-discipline. Do not associate with anyone who abuses drugs or themselves. That's my definition of a winner. When you associate yourself with one loser, you can never win. The person you choose cannot have an affliction that keeps them from being a positive force in society. So if you decide to choose losers to support you, then don't bother reading any more of what I've written. Don't waste others' time or your own. You're not ready to let go of your old ways yet. Be humble and give my writings to someone who is working hard to free their soul from their afflictions.

Now that you have the head of your support team and have confronted your demons or negative emotions, you're ready to move to the second application.

Application Two: Now it's time to pray. Pray to whomever or whatever your soul chooses. For me, it's the Holy Spirit. It will be different for each of you. It does not matter, as long as it is a positive energy. Your goal is to establish a positive energy deep within yourself where your soul exists.

Now you need to let go of everything and let God or this positive energy into your life wholeheartedly. Let this positive force be with you. This will create a covering to smother the wrong impressions in your mind and soul. Make sure this energy is something good and positive in your life. You have now learned how to give yourself a spiritual awakening.

Application Three: Get out of dodge. The positive winner you have chosen to lead your support team should be willing to help you. The amount of time you have been abusing yourself will determine the distance you'll have to move. Five years or less, I strongly recommend that you move a minimum of four hundred and fifty miles away. Five years or more, I strongly recommend that you move a minimum of nine hundred miles away. You will have to leave behind everyone you knew, whether they were a positive or negative influence in your life. Because you associated with negative influences to begin with, you have no control whatsoever over your choices or actions. You cannot remain in the same everyday environment you're in now. You won't be able to apply any more applications. You will fail every time.

Application Four: Reinvent yourself. Pick a new name or nickname. Pick one that you always wanted to be called. Guess what? It's who you're going to become in your new future. This person will strive to be positive and will have only positive, affliction-free friends. No one will know anything about your past unless you tell him or her. You can recreate yourself in this new location. Also, your supporter should put money back for you to purchase a round-trip ticket to your past place of abuse. I will elaborate more on that later in this guide. You now can be a positive person in your new environment with a new beginning.

What Have We Learned About How to Be a Success in Life so Far?

Application 1

We need to let go of our secrets and confront our demons. We must cut loose from our pasts, which are filled with negative memories, bottled up emotions, anxieties, depression, and other negative emotions that go on endlessly. With this Application, you have just given yourself a chance for a positive future that deep down you are seeking. This is the first application in helping to free your soul and to obtain winners in your life.

Application 2

Now you have to pray to whoever is of your choosing. Now you will create for yourself a window of opportunity through which the Holy Spirit, God, or whomever you choose will guide you. The window or wormhole effect will occur. All you have to do is crawl through it. By doing this, you will create a belief deep inside of your soul. You will now believe in yourself. People who believe in themselves can do anything they choose. Whomever you chose to pray to will love you to your own understanding. Now you will create a spiritual awakening.

You have also just learned that you have created a trust within your whole being, because you have to trust wholeheartedly in your choice in the first place. Remember, your heart is one of the closest entities to your soul. Through and through, you can't go wrong if you trust in whatever is of your choosing. You will establish a belief within yourself without question. If you don't believe in a positive force, then you cannot believe in yourself. So you cannot advance.

Application 3

You should also have learned by now, after repeating the same mistakes over and over, that you cannot remain in the same place. If this were not true, then you wouldn't be in the situation you're in at this very moment, and I wouldn't be writing this guide now. I'm helping you to see what I've seen myself.

After applying these first three applications to your new life, you're ready for another application:

the blueprint. You will have to create a blueprint or plan for your future.

Application 4

Pick a direction in which you want to move: north, south, east, or west. The length of time you've been abusing yourself will determine how far you will have to move. The minimum I recommend is four hundred fifty miles away from where you abused yourself. Next, you should change your name. Your new name will be who you will become. You should also have your supporter set back enough money for a round-trip ticket. I will explain more on this later.

After making the arrangements to move to where you have decided, you will have to segregate yourself from the abuse you inflicted upon yourself. You will need to be totally separated from your abuse. You will leave behind all the negativity from your past life style. At this moment, since you do not have control over your situation, you will have a rock bottom feeling that you will have to experience.

If you cannot find support or relocate at this time, don't think you are getting off that easy! HA! HA! I strongly recommend that you put yourself in the Salvation Army ARC. You will learn a lot about yourself as I did while I was there. You will also establish a good work ethic, patience, spirituality, a wardrobe, and a lot of forgotten morals and values. I did my dues. I spent a lot of time in the Salvation Army in St. Petersburg, Florida.

Important Information

Sick 'n tired of being sick 'n tired. WOW! That one phrase is so powerful, especially if you're living in a dismal hell that you created for yourself. This is one of many phrases that I learned from drug rehabilitation centers and from living on the streets. This phrase is one of many truths that you will come to know in time if you are abusing yourself.

Right now is the time for a new beginning for your soul's salvation. Don't look at the negative reasons why your life is dysfunctional or just in total despair. Focus on one positive thought that you can truthfully, without a doubt, say to yourself right now. "I'm not feeding my affliction at this time." "I'm on my way to being a winner." These are positive thoughts. Guess what? All of your doubts will disappear as you make and think about these positive choices.

Now, if you're in jail, obtain all the literature that you can that explains feelings and emotions. Remember that without understanding the whole problem the problem cannot be fixed. Educate yourself; after all, you only have precious time.

If you're in a rehabilitation center, then the literature and counselors are already around you. Don't be afraid to ask the counselors anything you want to know. There is no such thing as a wrong question, only ones you don't ask. Jails or treatment centers are your only two safe places if you cannot escape your environment. And in the blink of an eye time will pass, and then you'll be released.

If you just got out of jail or a rehabilitation center, then welcome to the free world in which I now live. One week before making this minimum four hundred-fifty-mile journey, you'll have to prepare yourself for whichever place you choose. You're going to have to line up a support group. You're going to need support constantly. Your support group should only be one or two people at first. You want to keep all the confusion to a minimum. Remember, you can only mimic winners right now.

Wherever you're going, you will need structure and a job. You cannot trust yourself with money at this time. You cannot handle money, an automobile, a jetliner, or a train. Guess what? You're starting all over again. That means that you will have to apply these applications yourself. There isn't any transportation that man makes that will get your soul to salvation. You have to crawl this crawl. Pray to whomever you believe in wholeheartedly and apply positive thinking. This will breed positive results and outcomes.

The people who love you -- parents, husbands, wives, brothers, sisters, and friends -- have also lived with your terrible curse. These people are hurting because they have had to exist inside the hell you created. They suffer too.

If you haven't experienced an affliction yourself, then you simply don't understand what the person you love is going through mentally. You only know what the ones you love have put you through. You're going to need time away from the person who has an affliction so you can start your own healing process. If you have stuck it out with someone who has an affliction because of your unconditional love for them, then you're most likely the only person that they feel they can trust. Unfortunately, you may have to let the one you love go. I know that it's tough, but it is what it is. It's the only way to help the person who is infected with afflictions.

Remember, any kind of love starts from deep within all of us. You have to love yourself before you will be capable of loving anybody or anything. Family and friends will still need to continue to support this person. All you can do at this point is to make sure whatever place the afflicted person decides to go is as pleasurable as possible for them. This person has to be in a less stressful environment than they were in previously. This is where you come in as a distant supporter, helping from afar to support them as they learn to stand on their own two feet again.

Now you, the one who previously abused yourself, has to make a pact. YOU CANNOT WHATSOEVER PARTICAPATE IN YOUR PAST AFFLICTIONS. This new place where you are living is your sanctuary! You know where you're at now at this very moment. You have the truths that I experienced myself over time and I know this to be reality.

Wherever you are, you will have your supporters control your earned money. Make sure that they make it possible for you to go back and forth daily to your new job. Now continue to live and go to work. Guess what? You are now living your life and crawling along the right route. So far, if you get what I'm writing then a great life is in store for you.

Footprints

Our emotions are like footprints imprinted deep in the snow. How do we erase these footprints that were created over time? We need fresh snow to cover over the previous footprints.

A footprint is nothing more than an impression left behind that lies deep within our soul. It can be due to lies, negative choices or thoughts, and so forth that we previously lived or told ourselves. Past afflictions can be changed. How? Well, by going back to the beginning and cutting loose the ties that bound your soul. You can change your behaviors. Remember this saying: life is hard to come, easy to go.

Starting over with truth, positive choices, positive thoughts, and positive people is what you have to do at this point. You will begin to rid yourself of afflicting behaviors. Remember, you're an infant again. I recommend from this point on you do all you can to live in a positive and just manner. When you do this, then automatically you will be on the positive route. Again, only you can crawl this crawl towards freeing your soul and covering up the previous footprints distilled deep within your soul.

Do you feel me? Bear with me; I'm not the best at this. I hope I'm not confusing you. If I am, then I'm sorry. It's not my intension to confuse you, but only to help you to see what I saw in myself. I want you to understand what you're dealing with.

Now we can begin your healing process. You can begin crawling towards that happy, joyous, and free route. If you're at this point, then you should be in your new environment and at the beginning of your new life with the supporter or supporters of your choice.

Remember, if you have been in a previous negative relationship, then you have to exit from that relationship. You can only stay in positive relationships. No Exceptions! If you hold on to your previous relationship that was or is negative, then all your hard work will end up being another unsuccessful attempt. On the other hand, if you're in a relationship that is positive with an affliction-free person, then you're lucky. If this person has stuck by you through thick and thin during the hard times of your afflictions, then this person probably believed in you even before you believed in yourself. This is a great person whom you should keep as one of your supports.

You should now start to mimic the ones who are supporting you. Mimic their every move. Remember, THEY CANNOT BE ONES WHOSE SOULS ARE CONSUMED OR HAVE BEEN CONSUMED BY THE SAME AFFLICTION AS YOU! The best candidate is a person who is living responsibly or one of the innocent people you dragged through the emotional mud with you. They are special because of their strength and the belief that you can change. Now remember, you are an infant again. You cannot make choices for yourself. The only choices you get to make are where you want to move, which is where you should be now, and the winner you choose to help you to change your life.

Demons

What are demons? Demons are nothing more than projections of our own worst fears, the fears from which we run away. Why is this? Why do we run away from our fears in the first place? We don't understand what we fear, so we try to escape it. We have fear of change itself. To change is to feel fear. It's hard to take action to make a change. Why? Because you're comfortable at this moment even if you're living a horrible existence.

It's easier to run away than to change willingly. Until you face your fears and learn to understand them, you will repeat the same mistakes over and over again. The term "addict" is a crutch that enables you to run in the first place. That is why after you have made the decision to better yourself that you should go into a residential treatment facility. Why a residential treatment facility, you're wondering?

- Because you separate yourself from your past abuses.

- There are counselors to talk to so you can deal with your fears and the sudden changes in your life.

- So you can learn to understand emotions and to identify new emerging feelings and mood swings.

- To give you time to set up a game

plan or blueprint for your new future.

- To collect as many tools as you can so you'll know what to do when the time comes to make the difference and avoid a relapse.

Now, don't carry any unnecessary baggage into your new life, especially past demons. You won't progress. That is why it is very important that you seek counseling to help you to understand your fears. Stop! Face your fears so you won't have any more demons haunting you. Counselors and your chosen winners will help you.

What You Should Have Obtained by Now

- You should have cut loose all the ties that bound your soul.

- You now have positive forces helping to guide you along with ONLY POSITIVE people as your main supporters.

- You should have obtained a job and structure along with outlets, which are people who are in your new everyday life. A good life requires hard work and consistency.

- You should now start crawling towards your new direction, which consists of your now being on the right route. Remember my saying! If you hang out with one loser, then you can never win.

- You should have now reinvented yourself into whatever name or personality you have chosen to become.

Understanding Emotions

What is an emotion? An emotion is a spawned pressure that is released in an instant due to one of your natural five senses. An unidentified emotion is an emotion that YOU DON'T UNDERSTAND.

You will probably be experiencing your first of many cravings right about now. The only thing that you should do right now is SLEEP! Sleep is a must and will enable you to move past your unexpected new set of cravings. Lots of sleep will help you to succeed in abstaining from your abuse.

Remember, you don't have the understanding of what you're dealing with yet. You are once again an infant and lack any understanding of society's standards. These standards or rules of society are the opposite of what you're used to living. Your self-afflicted lifestyle most likely had completely different rules. You used to be dependent on everything around you. You're beginning to change that now. Remember to keep everything around you simple. Let this unsuspecting life flow through you; exist in it instead of having it existing without you.

Don't worry about what you're experiencing right now. Remember, you may not understand what you're feeling yet. Let your support team deal with the standards or rules of society, such as paying bills, taxes and problems that arise due to your past lifestyle. That is why they're supporting you in the first place. If you get what I'm writing, then you will become a winner just like them.

You will be experiencing all kinds of unidentified emotions. You are probably having trouble dealing with them all, which could compromise your new set of balances. RELAX! It's okay! You should only deal with one and only one unidentified emotion at a time. It is easier to deal with one emotion than ten. "Me, myself, and I" have dealt with all of this already. I tried to understand one particular emotion at a time so I could turn that emotion from an unidentified emotion to an identified emotion.

What positive thing happened for me then? Well, I learned that I only had nine more unidentified emotions to learn. I learned everything that I could on the how and why of every emotion that was left. Eventually, I had no more unidentified emotions, only identified emotions that I had gotten past, and knew it because I was on a positive route.

What Was Easier for Me!

When I was feeling angry, depressed, anxious, or overwhelmed, I turned that negative emotional reaction around. I reacted to that negative emotion by acting on the opposite emotion. If I were angry, then I worked on being happy. I became passive instead of aggressive. I know doing this takes lots of practice and an unmeasured amount of time. We all, as human beings, have in each new moment a new beginning. Stop, seize the moment change your life.

You see, everything in life has an opposite that creates a balance to make life work. Now, out of an angry emotion or feeling, which is negative, I reacted with an opposite emotion of being happy to rid myself of the angry emotion or feeling. I realized from this point on that I could turn my behavior totally around. I was learning piece by piece how to deal with a negative emotion and how to turn that emotion into a positive emotion.

All my outcomes since have been positive ones, and all of your newfound results will be too.

My point is that you need to use an opposite action to a negative feeling to turn your negative into positive. This is your SOUL'S purpose. You'll be crawling on the positive route, teaching yourself how to become a positive human being rather than a negative one.

So what have we learned here? Well, we just learned how to deal with negative feelings and emotions. You will also realize piece by piece how to begin making good choices. This will indicate that you're on the right route. Also, you'll be teaching yourself how to be in control of your actions to unidentified emotions and feelings.

Well, you have been abstaining from your old habits for quite a while now and guess what? The phone is ringing with your old master from your past trying to call you. In other words, you're dealing with another craving, old bad memories, and lots of new negative feelings and emotions. This is to be expected because you have not learned enough about yourself and how to apply balances into your new life yet. All this you're experiencing right now will last for about a week, and then it will pass on by. Hopefully, you've made a positive change and moved yourself past this three-month craving. Remember, people and life itself will push your emotions and feelings to their limits. DO NOT ACT ON ANYTHING.

If all this new change becomes too difficult for you to handle in the free world, then go to the Salvation Army ARC or any other drug treatment center nearest to you as your new last resort. It all comes down to what we think of ourselves in the first place. Stop, seize the moment change your life. This starts immediately when your actions are the opposite of negative emotional reactions. Now you should have a solution on how to deal with your currently negative feelings and emotions.

After each of these three-month cravings pass, life should resume as it has for the previous three months, unless you went backwards by reintroducing yourself back to your previous afflictions. If you have, then you have. It is what it is. It's not the end of the world for you, but only the beginning. If you slipped, then guess what? You have to start over after coming back from your long down and out nine or four hundred-fifty-mile journey. Remember, YOU CANNOT PARTICAPATE IN YOUR PAST AFFLICTIONS AT ALL IN YOUR NEW ENVIRONMENT! If you do, then the new place you have established will be ended. You cannot remain in this newly tarnished environment. You will not progress in a forward direction. Your new hard-earned existence will become just another environment in which you're abusing yourself. Why leave your previous life in the first place? I strongly recommend that you go back to the front of this guide, read it again and start over. If you haven't resumed your past bad behavior, then let's go on.

By now, you should have positive people around you to feed from or mimic. Learn everything that there is to learn about those positive people. No matter if they are on TV, at your job, or new friends in your environment, they need to be a positive influence that you can talk to or be inspired by. You're creating a support group that you will need now that you are a child and no longer an infant.

You should be receiving more knowledge from whomever you worship. Ask now for more understanding of each and every new problem you've been dealing with. You should start building your mental strengths. Another positive thing that you'll come to realize is that you haven't been participating in your previous afflictions. You also have established a belief within yourself. After all, you're not living in your past, but living towards your new future.

Boundaries

Now more than ever, you're going to set boundaries for yourself and those around you to follow. What is a boundary? A boundary is a perimeter that you surround yourself with mentally and physically.

This boundary will help you avoid negative influences. It can be a square, rectangle, circle, or whatever you fancy. These boundaries that you set for yourself and others CANNOT be crossed. You must stay within your boundaries at all times, and others must understand and respect the boundaries you have set for yourself.

If you do not respect the boundaries and participate with even just one loser, it will keep you weak. If you let a loser within your boundaries, you run the risk of having an unsuccessful result. Some examples of boundaries you may set for yourself are as follows:

- I must go to work and then right home, unless I am with my supporter.

- I cannot talk to any of my old party friends or anyone who may bring up emotions that may trigger a craving or desire for my old self-destructive behavior.

- I cannot act immediately on an emotion.

- I cannot have access to more than twenty dollars at any given time.

These are just a few boundaries that you can set for yourself that will help you to stay on the right path. You may add to these boundaries as you identify things that cause you to want to return to your old destructive life style.

Even I have people from my past that do not understand why I can never talk to them. They just don't get it. The only thing they know is that we were party friends for many years, and now I won't talk to them. That is because they are losers who are still spinning their wheels by doing the same old things. I don't want to live that life anymore. I have set my boundaries and moved forward. So can you.

What Is Choice?

Choice is an entity that determines the outcome of your future. Positive choices equal a positive future. Negative choices equal a negative future. Do you see how you make the difference in your life depending on the choices you make throughout time?

Also, what you tell yourself will make the difference in how strong your belief system is in yourself. Now, recite this to yourself, "My future depends on all the choices I will make and actions I will take to change my own destiny."

You are the only human being that can do this for yourself. No one else can do it for you. You will now be moving with time itself, moment by moment, not time moving without you, passing you by.

Now, if you understand what I've been writing so far, you're ready to start setting small, achievable goals. You see, you hold the key for achieving anything that you believe in. If you believe it, you can create it.

Combining Your Character

Right now, it's about building your new character. You should be combining your new character with your new self-chosen name. This name is the one that you've given yourself in this new life you're now living. By combining everything you have learned about yourself with your new name, you have created the new person that you're going to become. By now you should have completely cut off the last of your lingering past and set yourself on the right route.

Now you should simply let your new life take its course, good, bad, or indifferent. Remember that repairing something of this magnitude is a difficult task because of all the footprints left behind deep within your soul from all the previous abuse we inflicted upon ourselves. You can erase these old negative memories. How? By newly created positive memories. Erasing old negative memories takes an unmeasured amount of time. Don't rush things. In time you will understand. Also, do not keep score on your transition. Just keep moving forward with your new life.

Keeping score or counting days is like watching a clock. Time goes by really slowly, which spawns negative emotions. The two most common negative emotions are depression and irritability. This will compromise everything, even the results of your hard-earned future. It's simple: there is no token or award for your abstinence. You're living the award. You're away from your afflictions, living out the character you have chosen to become.

Building your new character will help the outcome of your future. My self-chosen name is Rich. Rich is also the character that I became. After time passed, I became someone that exceeded my own expectations. One never knows who they really are until they give themselves a chance to become the person they totally believe they can be.

I believe in my new self one hundred percent. We never know our own capabilities until WE PUT OURSELVES to the test. Again, you're living your new life, which severs all your past ties. So again, my point is to not count the days going by or keep score, because this will cause depression. You could ultimately cause yourself not to focus on the life that you're living now. You could find that you might have to face negative results. All right, then; let us move on.

By now you should be on your new schedule of going back and forth to work and then heading straight home. You will automatically start a routine that will create structure, which will keep your transition simple. What you're doing at this point is nothing more than a transition to your new life.

Now you'll go to about your sixth month and then cravings may surface again. A craving may come to you in a dream. For me, they were what I called "crack dreams." Now you're going to be faced with the possibility of going backwards again. This means resuming your old negative ways and possibly living them out.

Remember the money your supporter put back to purchase a round-trip ticket to your past place of abuse. Well, guess what? You're going to need that money for that ticket. If you make it past this six-month craving, then you're right where you're supposed to be. Keep up the good work.

However, if you don't make it, then hanging on to the life you're living now will become very dismal. You are probably out of control and looking to argue and fight with everyone for an excuse to run away. You are looking for an excuse to run right back to your old stomping grounds and afflictions. At this time you should use the money, buy the ticket and get it out of your system. Then after this slip you need to get right back on that plane and start all over again.

After passing my six-month cravings, I managed to hold onto my new life for two more months. Then the worst happened. I went on a nine hundred mile journey back to living out my old ways with crack cocaine. I can honestly say from my standpoint now that this slip was a normal and positive thing in several ways.

One, I realized that I went eight months not participating in my previous afflictions. Second, I observed that my rekindled love affair wasn't the same as it had been before I moved nine hundred miles away. Third, I realized that I had the ability to get back to my new positive life. Fourth, I truthfully knew that I had never been high on crack in Maryland, the state that had become my refuge.

You see, I'd set up a structured life by going

back and forth to work and NOT PARTICAPATING in negative influences, which would have caused me to tarnish the sanctuary that I'd worked so hard for in Maryland. For those eight months before my slip I experienced life, as I never had before. I decided to resume my new life because I'd gotten a taste of what a real life was. I had lived a new life with promise. Plus, I'd accumulated achievable goals that I wanted to achieve. All of your hard-learned lessons will pay off eventually. Once you receive knowledge of this, then you'll know that it will be easier to come back to your chosen sanctuary of your own free will. Remember, if you haven't slipped yet; stay on the current path you're on. You're doing better than I did myself. You're ahead of the pack.

But if your results are the same as mine, I will tell you when you get back from your trip to keep everything simple. Resume living your previous schedule. Now, you'll have to establish balances in your new beginning. Remember, you're an infant again being reborn as every moment passes. All life on earth is momentary with NO EXEPTIONS! Remember my saying: Stop, seize the moment change your life.

If you slip you will now be an infant again just starting to crawl. An infant will fall many times before they walk. So don't let what happened haunt you. It's only your past demons surfacing because you stirred things up by reliving your past afflictions. This too shall pass. Keep that phrase in your mind constantly, especially during the new growing pains that you will have to go through.

The things that you have to do at this point, after being strong enough to come back, is to heal yourself physically and mentally. Don't think about yesterday because -- you know what? It's passed on, and so have you. Don't feed into the negative slander because of your relapse. The people around you and those you're involved with in your sanctuary -- outside of your chosen supporters -- don't have a clue about your relapse in the first place. Only people from your past will slander you because of your slip. They don't want to see you succeed because they still exist in misery or feel you have wronged them in your past afflictions.

If people in your sanctuary don't ask, then simply don't tell. They are just everyday people around you. These people DON'T CARE ABOUT YOU FOR YOU. So they don't care to learn about your triumphs or past relapse. Only those who are supporting you are the people who truly care. The only friends that you should have are the winners supporting your best interest. Everyone else is nothing more than acquaintances. In other words, don't make friends with just anyone. The ones you choose have to be winners. NO EXCEPTIONS. Now, once again, you'll be on the right route, moving forward instead of backwards.

Now it's time to get in touch with your surroundings, meaning nature. Watch animals, birds, or anything living outdoors in nature. Study everything that you see. Why? Because this will give you more lessons about natural balance. You see, the first eight months of your new life you could only concentrate on acquiring support, structure, and balance. You only learned the basics of life and society's standards with your newly invented self. Now you will become one with the earth itself. Watching animals will give you understanding about the natural balance of life and how it works. It works believe me! Why? Animals are smarter than we are, in the first place. They are not being corrupted by anything. Everything that animals do is based on a natural lifestyle with balances. The Animal Planet Channel is a great start for you because this channel shows the natural balances of nature itself.

Time is going to pass again, and guess what? Everything that you've had to go through in the time before your slip is going to emerge again. Keep in mind that you've already established a belief in yourself because you have already passed through all this before. If you've done it once then you will do it again automatically. So, guess what? If you believe in yourself, you can do anything.

Now you're going to create a direction for yourself, your dreams, and higher goals. You will have to work hard toward the goals you set for yourself. In time, these goals and higher goals will eventually turn into your dreams, which you are working so hard to accumulate.

Dreams

What are dreams? Dreams are nothing more than desires that stem from your preferences and your belief system. Having faith and believing in yourself you can achieve your dreams, no matter how farfetched they are. You see, it's like an empty glass that's sitting on top of a table. The glass represents the world in which you seek. Next, you have the ingredient of water. The water represents your actions, hard work, determination, and what you want out of life. It's your goals and dreams that you haven't achieved yet.

Now, it comes down to the ultimate question of how to achieve all those farfetched dreams and goals. Having a belief within yourself in those dreams and goals is one of the keys to your achieving them. Achieving your dreams depends on how much water you're willing to put in the glass to fill it up. It all comes down to you.

You are the one with the answers to the questions you ask about how to achieve your dreams. That is why you must surround yourself with winners, because winners will lead you down the road to your dreams. Achieving your goals and dreams depends on how much faith you have in your beliefs.

Now that we have established that you have the knowledge of how to achieve your dreams and goals, you're going to need inspiration, foresight, and a focus point for your dreams. Whether it's a fancy car, airplane, family, or a home you want, inspiration starts with a magazine or a camera. Obtain as many pictures as you can of your new life's good memories, goals, and dreams. Place all of these pictures where you're going to spend a great deal of your day. Look at these pictures that you have taken or cut out of a magazine every day. Guess what? You're now moving towards obtaining your dreams and goals. Bet you didn't even know it.

The majority of human beings believe only in what they see. A perfect example of this is the old adage, "Seeing is believing." Guess what? Believe it, because you're achieving your dreams and goals the instant you hang your pictures. Your pictures will keep your mind focused on what you're achieving. This will give you direction as to where and how far you want to go in your new life. Remember that learning all this takes time. There is no pill you can take that will relieve the growing pains you face. Relax! Don't make any choices on your own right now. Your choices are all compromised because of your previous slip. If you have slipped, then you should only exist with your supporters' help and their help alone.

I advise you now to get a cat. This is a true story. I didn't like cats; I liked dogs. But I ended up with this feral kitten that was very young. He was born in the neighbor's bushes and spent his first few weeks of life doing all he could to survive during a heavy Maryland snowfall. When I first saw him, he was the only kitten that did not run away. He ran towards me sideways, hissing and spitting. Then he stopped and walked right up to me. He looked up at me as if to say, "What are you waiting for? Take me home. It's cold and lonely out here." So I did. He was as cute as can be and loved me unconditionally, but the little guy was born with what looked like a protruding belly button or a cyst on his abdomen. I knew from that moment that I'd have to stop thinking just about my problems and myself. I was now faced with unfamiliar problems and realizations. I knew that this kitten would die if I didn't accept him. Well, being the person I had become, I decided to take on these unfamiliar problems.

I had been saving and working towards one of my goals, a 1998 Dodge Ram 1500 four-wheel drive pickup truck. That goal would soon be put on hold. I found out that the cute little bulge on my kitty's belly was a herniated belly button, and his intestines were being strangled.

You see life itself has its own plan for us all. Sometimes things we plan or are counting on don't unfold as fast as we'd like or the way we would like. All we can do is have patience and not resist the flow of life, but accept it. I am suggesting that you get a cat because you will fall in love with it, and it will love you back. It will teach you not to be as selfish as you were in your old life. The cat will depend on you for its survival, and you will start to learn about responsibility piece by piece.

Remember that the one you pray to is the force that's guiding you. After letting go of your secrets in the very beginning, you started praying to the entity that gives you your strength. For me, it is the one I call the Holy Spirit.

You're now going toward the direction of success while grasping at living a happy life. It's the opposite of the way you used to live when you were abusing yourself. Hopefully, you're starting to understand the whys of what I've written so far. If you're living happily instead of sadly, then you already know you're on the right route and on your way to living a successful life. See? You are starting to think positively.

Anyway, I ended up using most of the truck money my supporter was holding for me to save my kitten. The Holy Spirit had other plans for my money and me. I was faced with a choice that I believe to this day was a test from the Holy Spirit to see what I would do. I chose to save that kitten's life. That choice was an unselfish choice. It was a hard choice, since I'd been saving for my goal for what seemed like forever.

My truck became a farther-off dream than originally planned as I spent every penny I had to save my kitten. I did not even hesitate when the vet told me that it was in a bad place and that he only had a 50/50 chance of surviving. It did not matter. I had worse odds than that against me, and I was surviving. I had to give this kitten the same chance. I am glad to say that it was worth it, and to this day my cat is a loving, nonjudgmental companion.

Well, guess what? I was now faced with more unfamiliar problems. After my kitten's being released from the veterinarian with a successful operation, I found myself almost broke. Yes, this kitten depended on me. *Who am I?* I thought. *Well, I guess I'm a new father.* You see, I learned that if you have only one supporter, eventually a normal person is going to grow tired of hearing you vent daily. Believe me, you will vent a lot. The animal of your choosing will not care if you vent to them. This will keep unexpected pressures due to anxieties at a minimum. Yes, you and that animal will no doubt become the best of friends over time. Animals don't voice opinions on what you're saying. They just listen. You will need that support you know. You will need for someone to listen to all of your anxieties without casting judgment on what you say.

You should now have a positive animal that needs you as well as people who are positive. Now I'm going to teach you how the United States post office can help you. Because of their ability to deliver mail, you can give your animal a break from your venting. No matter what you're feeling, write your feelings down on paper. Why? So you can observe your own behavior. Mail your unidentified emotions and feelings to yourself. You see, you have to write all the truths of how you're feeling for this to work.

Collect these envelopes that contain your emotions and feelings you felt when you wrote them. Do not open them until you want to go backwards to your old existence. Then open them and read them before you go back. You will see how much you've changed since you wrote these feelings down. I guarantee you won't feel the same feelings or emotions as you did when you wrote them earlier. Read your writings and simply learn by them.

You will find you have given yourself a timeline to knowing the next time you might slip due to negative feelings and emotions. Take heed of this lesson and strengthen yourself during or around the date of your first writing next year. You'll be able to understand your emotions better after reading your writings. You can detect which negative emotions or feelings you can turn around, send away or change into positive ones.

This exercise will help you in the long run to become a winner. As time passes by, understanding of your previous problems and afflictions will increase as your negative mindset becomes less and less powerful. You see, a new life will eventually take over your past one. You will find that your previous problems due to your past afflictions won't apply to you as much in your new life. You are living in the here and now along with your supporters and your animal.

In case you slip, the animal you choose should be a low-maintenance animal, an animal that you don't have to take outside regularly. Your animal should be able to protect and feed itself as long as it has enough food and water. But I recommend that you obtain an animal ONLY IF YOU ARE LIVING WITH A SUPPORTER so the animal can be totally protected. That's the benefit I received by having a cat and a few supporters.

Responsibility and How to Obtain It

To obtain responsibility, you need help from your supporter. You have to start learning how to pay your own bills with the money that you earn honestly. Rent, food, oral hygiene products, and your way back and forth to work, etc. These are the essential basics. By taking care of your animal, you will automatically learn how to take care of yourself and fulfill other types of responsibilities. Remember to mimic your supporters. They have been helping you to help yourself since your departure.

You see, I was a chronic cocaine abuser who supported my affliction from hour to hour twenty-four hours a day seven days a week. That was along with other afflictions that I lived out for twenty-three years straight due to negative choices and actions that I created long ago. Two years after my move, I realized that I had only slipped a few times. Comparing that to how much I used to abuse myself, I knew through and through that I was living towards a positive future in which I would be affliction-free.

After you become more responsible, like paying your bills without the help of your supporters, you will begin to feel a sense of self worth. It's up to you how much self worth you create for yourself. Checks and balances are the main fuel on how much self worth will be obtained. You will need to apply different balances in your life to enable your transition to become doable and desirable.

Keep yourself in check. Repairing past afflictions of this magnitude is always going to be tough. Time is the main ingredient that will change you automatically, along with brand new moments of natural life experiences. The progression will take you in a different direction mentally.

Bits and pieces of your dignity will be established again. No matter what kind of job you've had to obtain as long as it is an honest job you will eventually win. You will again become a responsible human being instead of an irresponsible one. Remember that if you hang out with one loser you can never win. Don't associate yourself with people who are irresponsible. These people will in fact hold you back by their influence alone.

Understanding Progressive Habits

Everything to start with is progressive, especially habits. Progressive habits are nothing more than an accumulation of different afflictions. These afflictions become a main part of our lives, good, bad, or indifferent. We take them to the extreme, to the point that these introduced afflictions or habits start gradually to become a part of our everyday lives.

This is my own definition of progressive habits. I learned through unmeasured amounts of time that all progressive habits can be changed by reintroducing positive new balances and habits into your current life. This will create a life that's doable to your own understanding. For example, when I started to become bored with my current life, job, and home and society's standards, etc., I introduced new additions into my life, like writing, inventing things, gardening, etc. These new additions or balances will teach you responsibility and help you get past boredom.

Remember, all habits are gradual. If you like plants or gardening, then I recommend that you watch *Yard Crashers* on DIY or HGTV. Why? Because these channels, along with others will teach you new hobbies that always come out beautifully. If you like to do construction, then I recommend *Holmes on Homes*. You will be able to introduce new hobbies that you can do to dissipate your boredom.

Understanding Time Itself

Time is the entity in which everything on earth exists moment by moment. Past, present, and future are time itself. When you make the most of your time, you will create balances and moments that will help your life to even itself out in a positive way. You have to seize the moment that you exist in to change your future. NO EXCEPTIONS! Your past is irrelevant. The present time you're living now makes new moments that separate your present from your past. A moment is the past, present, and future all moving constantly and simultaneously. You should be able to change the moment to change your future. Remember, your final action to any of your emotional reactions at any given moment is the key to securing a positive future.

Time constantly moves forward as it has since the beginning of the earth. No human being can stop this movement forward. But the direction of the moment we can control. You must learn to control the direction if you want to move with time itself from one moment to the next. I call this living in the moment and for the moment. This is what I'm in now. I live in the blessing in which I've been given, a moment's worth of time, a moment to relish all that I can that is broken down to a mere action to a reaction, then to a choice that I am in control of at this very instant.

Do you see where I'm going with this? We all have control over this entity. Don't be fooled by thinking that you don't have control over your life's direction, no matter how vulnerable you seem to be because of your situation. *This too shall pass.* All things, situations, so forth and so on always do. Keeping this phrase in mind assures that you will have something to believe in as well as in yourself.

Again, anything in life starts out with a belief. This is the main vehicle in getting any human to their destination, no matter where you want to arrive. Faith secures the fuel that you'll need to arrive at the destination you believe in whole-heartedly. Without total belief and faith in anything, you WON'T move forward. You WILL be negatively grounded – done! -- Never going anywhere or doing anything differently. Remember, if nothing changes, then, simply that: nothing changes. My point is to change your moment.

Labeling Yourself

What is labeling your self? It is nothing more than what you tell yourself. AA, NA, CA, and all affiliates are usually based on twelve-step programs. These facilities mostly want to help people free themselves from the despair in which they are living. Meetings are great for alcoholics in AA because of the doctors who originally created the treatment program. You have to understand that these men who started AA lived through all of the growing pains and problems of alcoholism themselves. They experienced all of the negative effects and outcomes of their own problems and alcoholism.

Alcoholics formed Alcoholics Anonymous to help others who share their same problems of alcohol abuse. To start with, alcoholism is a social problem. When people drink, they gather around a bar, table, and so forth. People share their problems and life's current events while consuming alcohol. I only know this from hanging in a bar for thirteen years straight. I was only an observer because I have never been an alcoholic. I don't drink alcohol. I don't understand alcoholism as much as an alcoholic could. But what I do know is that AA meetings are the treatment of choice for their problem.

When I was going to countless NA meetings, I learned something about how you think about yourself. I discovered that when it was my turn to speak, I addressed myself as an addict. Think about it! What does that really mean? What are you telling yourself? I'm more than sure that I referred to myself as an addict on many occasion. Guess what? You are who you believe you are. I was confirming the negative result and negative consequences.

By saying that word to yourself, you have lessened the chance of overcoming the problem that you're faced with or attempting to correct. You see, when saying you're an addict, you've just created a label for yourself. Don't be fooled by this negative label because labeling yourself has repetitive negative consequences. Don't get confused by what I'm writing. Meetings are good if they help you to help yourself. If your life is better than what it was, then I encourage you to keep attending them. But unfortunately for most people, the negative labeling doesn't help with their self-esteem.

People create their own labels in life by confirming who they are and what they have done previously. An example is their choice of the word "addiction," which is a term I don't like to use. You don't need to admit repeatedly that you have an affliction. If you're not participating in an affliction at this moment, then you're not afflicted at this moment. You are affliction-free. If you are abusing yourself, then you will constantly repeat the same negative behaviors. Think about it. What is the definition of insanity? Doing the same thing over and over again and expecting a different result. What I'm saying is, if you keep slipping over and over, then try something new. If you don't, then nothing will change. Remember, if nothing changes, then simply that: nothing changes! Then all your hard work will become nothing more than repetitive attempts with no movement toward the positive. You see, you don't have to admit to yourself repeatedly that you have an affliction. Why? Because you have already established that, so what's to admit? You would just be reinforcing a negative movement in your life.

What is there to gain by referring to your self as an addict? You should only care about what you think of yourself and not about what other people think of you. These people do not know you on a personal level. Remember, the politics of anything is in everything. I believe that meetings are good for you only if you're in a residential treatment facility. Why? The topics that are shared in meetings sometimes become triggers. This can lead to cravings which can send you mentally back to your past afflictions when living outside on your own. In treatment centers, all the literature, tools, and support are around you constantly to help with your cravings.

A Sword

What is a sword and how does this term apply? A sword is nothing more than a weapon that we choose to use in battle. This applies to all of us, due to the vices that we have chosen. These vices will eventually end the existence of who we used to be and who we would have become, always ending negatively. "Those who live by the sword die by the sword" (Matt 26:52). Crack abuse equals death. Unprotected sex equals disease, unwanted pregnancy, etc. Anything that you do dishonestly will lead to a negative outcome and possibly death.

Positive influences are the only way to keep such things from happening to you. That is why it is important to mimic the supporters that you have chosen. Remember, in this battle you only have yourself. Well, I hope I'm getting you to see the truths of things. You see, the truth will set you free every time without a doubt.

I can tell you that for the eight years since I changed my life, I have been off crack for six years going on seven. I'm living life, a really great one, a life that is totally positive. I've done everything that I have written in this guide. Since the beginning of my affliction and throughout all my past attempts I have never had this amount of success in abstaining from crack, meth, and opiates. I know that everything that I'm writing works because every day I live in a great environment. I have my spirituality and, most importantly, myself. I have one hundred percent control of my choices and actions.

So which pill are you going to take the red one or blue one? Every guide needs a little humor. You know what people say: humor brings happiness your way. Smile, it's not that bad. Life goes on with you in it, and you can be anything you want if you believe, so believe.

Now I'll ask you: "What do you want to be when you grow up?" Answer the question to yourself. I can pretty much assume that the answer to that question was positive, wasn't it? You didn't say to yourself that you wanted to be something negative, did you? When asked that question you didn't think or believe for one moment that you wanted to be a loser or chose having afflictions as your career path. Do you see how looking at something shows you that you already have the control to change something from a negative to positive? Negative power is nothing but a waste of energy. So guess what? The car radio won't work on negative power. But positive power will power the whole car, not just the radio. So apply this to yourself and see what you come up with. I guarantee that if you feed from positive power, then you will be what you're feeding from: raw positive power.

This force can do anything. It can even move mountains. Take the moon, for instance, a farfetched dream. When you ask people if they believe that it's possible to go to the moon, most will in fact tell you yes without a doubt. Why is that? It's because they have seen and heard it before. It's after the fact. Yes, man did land on the moon. So the answer to that question is yes without a doubt. Ask the same question before man had landed on the moon and the responses would probably be, "You're crazy", "It's impossible," and, "Man can't land on the moon."

You see, the same question asked at different times gives the people responding two different trains of thought. My point is that before man landed on the moon that farfetched dream sounded impossible. Only the people having this dream believed in themselves enough to land on the moon eventually and make history. This only confirms that you are who you believe you are, which includes all of your dreams. Yes, your life can become positive and true along with your dreams no matter how farfetched they seem. You hold the key. You can achieve the dreams you believe in for yourself. All other dreams will follow in time. You just have to believe in what you're working towards with all of your heart. Again, your heart is the entity closest to your soul.

What I Have Done to Train my Eyes & Mind

What you're going to need now is: Two paper towel rolls.

Take the two empty paper towel rolls and hold them up to your eyes, creating a tunnel vision effect. Start to think about something you believe in; focus in that direction inside of your mind. This is important because over time looking at life through the paper towel rolls will teach your thoughts to align with your vision. You will be training your mind to learn how to focus on what's in your sights. As well as helping you focus on one direction without looking off into another. You will see the difference in your sights instantly.

I'll tell you how I can prove it. Hold the paper towel rolls like glasses in your hands. Yes, they look dorky and crazy. It's to be expected. Then look at a tree or an object that is a considerable distance away without the paper towel rolls. Empty your mind and focus on what you are looking at. Then say to yourself, "Tree", "Car," or whatever you're staring at while putting the paper towel glasses up to your eyes and look at the same object. Then walk over to the object or picture and touch it. You see instantly that the paper towel glasses gave you a different view of the same object. It also gives your eyes a tunnel vision effect that slows down time itself while your mind is concentrating on your goal. This, in fact, makes it easier to stay focused during your walk toward the object. Why? You only saw the direction in which you wanted to go: towards the objective. Then by touching the object, you establish a belief that you can obtain the object for yourself. It is now within arm's length. The point of this exercise is to teach you how to combine your mind and sight so they focus on one thing or belief together.

Remember earlier when I suggested that you hang a picture of your dreams up so you can see them every day? The glasses are good for looking at all those different dreams with tunnel vision as well, confirming an endless world of possibilities that you make possible. Seeing is believing and the things you see you believe. The glasses enable you to see only what you're looking at in that particular dream. You learn to believe in and focus on your dreams.

The good news is that once, in your past, you were abusing yourself. Now you are not. Before you focused only on your afflictions with which you abused yourself. Now you are focusing on positive things and dreams.

Positive & Negative Energy

A negative but positive fact of our past abuses is that it gave us ambition, dedication, strife, and that desire or hunger in which to feed our abuses. Failing to feed our abuses was not an option in our old lives. You see, you are already ahead of the pack. Believe it. The struggles, despair, aggravation, and depression that we had to go through have made us stronger than most everyday people. It's true.

With that fact uncovered, if you're changing your life for the positive, then you will surpass most people if you tap into that drive. Use that same drive/determination to reach your positive goal. You will achieve your dreams depending on how hungry you are and what you desire.

Now that you're living your first dream or goal of not participating in your past afflictions, you can start to work towards other dreams that you want. Again, you can achieve any goal or dream as long as you believe in yourself and in that dream.

Let's look at positive and negative energy. Positive energy is a force that empowers the world in which we live. Negative energy is nothing more than a ground. Period! Both energies are the basis of which planet earth consists. These energies are two different directions, but make up one natural balance. These two energies are part of what balances the world in which we live.

For example, you're sitting in a hot car with

the windows rolled up. You are sweating and uncomfortable. This controls your mood in a negative sense. But by using positive power or turning on your air conditioner, you don't have to be in despair any longer. The more positive power the car can give you, the more luxuries you're going to have. When you turn the air on, all the despair and negative emotions are taken away. Why? It's because of the positive power alone.

The rules are simple. Being positive gives you more luxuries, ends despair, negative feelings, and emotions. This will give your new environment meaning. It also makes your car a more pleasant place for you to be in. Once again, negative power is nothing more than a ground. So, guess what? If you feed from negative power then you won't have added luxuries. Your journey will always be miserable and negative. My point is to feed from positive energy and you will think positively, making you a positive person.

When you were feeding your afflictions, meaning everything in your past existence, it was nothing but negative. Remember, if you're feeding from a negative existence, then you yourself will be nothing more than what you are eating. This all stems from only one negative choice.

You have to cut your whole past loose and change from a negative to a positive. Your new life will automatically take you in a different direction. Life itself will teach you the lessons that will change your life from negative to positive. This will stem from your own will to survive in a different environment. You will automatically adapt by your natural instincts. You have to act with a positive action, due to a negative reaction, due to a negative choice, therefore changing negative to positive.

Balances

What are balances? Balances are nothing more than a group of additions or changes that makes your life work equally. Remember, everyone is different, so everybody's balances are different. It depends on a person's situation. The better your situation, the fewer balances or changes you're going to have to apply in your new life.

Everyone creates balances on their own to keep the flow of their life. Remember, without balances a negative result will occur. After all, balances create an equal structure. Structure is just a bunch of different balances to which you conform to make your life prosperous. Balance itself is nothing more than change, which minimizes life's problems.

For example, take an ordinary homemaker. They have to make lunch for their children, making sure the children eat and go to school. They have to pay bills, grocery shop, etc. Then they have to deal with spouses when they come home. You see this homemaker has created these balances that make life work. These balances turn into structure. If one balance were off, then their life would change. They have created their own set of balances, which makes life work in a positive manner.

Result: a homemaker who is happy. They'll be happier when their spouse comes home and tells them how much they appreciate them. Bring home a gift for their spouse or children. By doing this at the end of the day everyone will be happier. Now everyone will have a new positive beginning.

Moments

What is a moment? A moment is time that moves constantly and forever in one direction. That direction is forward. You see life exist in only a moment. Your life, my life, and all life on earth only exist momentarily. A moment is nothing more than a mere reflection or increment of time itself. Your past is nothing more than a mere moment frozen within your mind. Memories are reflected into your present living moment.

Letting go of the negative memories is only one of the requirements in achieving a positive life. How do we let go of our past no matter what our past contains? By changing the moment we are in now. This will change all of the moments that are to come.

You have the ability to change the future itself. I myself believe that anything is possible by observing time itself. Each and every human being is traveling through time. We do this constantly, moment by moment, through every life experience. Take me for instance. I have traveled for forty-five years through time. By looking at myself I can see that my reflection isn't the same as it was when I was younger. My years of traveling through time have changed me.

So yes, without a doubt we have traveled through time. We have moved through the past to the present, but not into the future. Our future can only be decided through our choices in the present. What you decide in the present moment will affect the moments to come, which are your future. Seize the moment; change your life and change your destiny.

Now, I ask you. What do you think the first clock was? It was a sundial that displayed the time. Since its invention long ago time has been measured by the balance of darkness and light, this is what gave our life structure. It helped create a time frame and a natural boundary that human beings could live within. Yes, a simple sundial enabled human beings not only to tell the time, but also to segregate morning, afternoon and night for a structured environment. We then could account for how much time went by during the changing seasons. All life on planet earth is supported by a single moment's worth of time itself.

Success

What is success? How do you know success after obtaining it? What is the difference, and why is it so important to have the wisdom to know the difference? Let's start with my definition of success: total happiness within your whole heart and one's own self is true success or happiness. How do you know success after obtaining it? By how happy you are inside and out. What is the difference, and why is it so important to know the difference? Many people rate success by how much money they earn. This is a fallacy. You cannot judge success by money. Why? Because, as I've learned myself, money comes and money goes, which makes basing success on money a non-supportive foundation.

The person makes the person. The person can rise up and make the money that they desire or require.

If you live your life in a just and honest manner, then by just and honest hard work will come a long-term, successful life. Once you have learned this lesson and practice it constantly, you will find that other successes will follow in suit one after the other. You have to keep the faith and believe in yourself.

You get to reinvent who you want to become now and in the future. Remember, letting go of your past is nothing more than living new life experiences. Once you decide to change completely, you will have a true taste of life itself. Living your life with you in it will help you to decide your own fate and change your destiny. You have that power now in this moment and this moment alone. So what's stopping you? Could it be you?

My Rules of Thumb

1) If nothing changes then simply that, nothing changes.

2) If you hang out with one loser, then you can never win.

3) You are who you believe you are.

4) If it's not meant to go into your body, then simply don't put it in there.

5) Believe in yourself and keep the faith.

6) Your choices determine your future.

7) True successes are within you.

8) Be happy with your whole self wholeheartedly.

9) Your actions determine all truths.

10) Be in the moment that you want to be.

11) Don't look back.

12) Stop, seize the moment change your life.

13) What you tell yourself makes all the difference.

14) Non-compliance of anything equals negative outcomes.

15) Stop death and destructive mindsets, bad attitudes, and resistance.

16) You are the creator and the creation of your own world.

17) Definition of character is defined by your actions.

18) If you believe it then you can create it.

19) Before anything can be achieved, it must first be created.

Your Choice of Actions

All life experiences evolve from your choice of action, good, bad, or indifferent. It depends on what action you choose to follow. Every choice of action since your birth has consequences, or a debt, if you will. But positive choices have no debt whatsoever, only successes, one right after the other. It all depends on the choices that you make.

You make the decision on how much you will pay in life due to the consequences of your actions. Negative actions equal negative consequences. Positive actions equal positive rewards. Do you see how you can make the difference?

For example, you make a negative choice to get high. You drive yourself to the dope hole. Then you buy fifty dollars worth of dope. You then make your way down the street when the unbelievable happens. You get pulled over. The police officer searches your vehicle and finds the dope you stashed. Now you're on your way to jail. Your choice to get high was a negative choice to begin with. Your choice of action to travel down to the dope hole was your negative action. The consequence for your choice of action to the negative choice is that now you're on your way to jail. The debt incurred by your negative choice of action is loss of yourself, your freedom, your vehicle and a guaranteed future financial burden.

You see, you dictate your own future by your actions due to your own choices. How could you have changed the outcome of all this in the first place?

DO NOT ACT ON NEGATIVE CHOICES. Remember, it's no crime by man's standards to have negative choices, only negative actions to those choices. Again, seize the moment; change your life. You make the difference.

Why Meetings Didn't Work for Me

I went to meetings constantly and repeated all my previous mistakes over and over again with always the same results: a lack of success. Why? By attending the meetings, I surrounded myself with negative people. If one person comes to the meeting from off the dirty streets, then negative emotions are stirred deep within our minds. Negative reactions, then negative choices left me with a negative action.

People believe that meetings are totally positive, but they are not. There are serious people in meetings who will abstain from abusing themselves, and then there are those who don't give a crap. Usually the people who don't care are losers by action. They have negative reactions, which lead to their negative choices and then definitely to a negative action.

Remember, if you hang out with one loser, then you can never win. There are people who only have small amounts of time clean since their last self-abuse. Those people believe through and through that they have all the answers. They don't. They are just on a power trip. This is why meetings did not work for me.

Meetings also didn't work for me because I learned that you have to leave your past behind you. I would listen to others' abuse stories and start thinking about my own abuses. This would actually trigger a craving, which would lead to a negative reaction. That's when I would choose a negative action, resulting in a negative choice. It had become an automatic response in my life.

Habits by Invitation

After moving to your new environment you'll have to look out for new habits. These habits will invite themselves into your life if you're not careful. Your personality is compromised due to your past abuse. When you overindulge in any particular habit, that habit will turn into a current affliction that you'll live out on a daily basis. My habit by invitation is coffee and cigarettes.

I found myself totally consumed in these afflictions. I realized that it was similar to my crack cocaine abuse. Caffeine in large doses will cause you to become easily irritable and angered with erratic behavior. My point is not to invite new habits into your new life, especially cigarettes and coffee or any caffeine product in large doses. It will become a new affliction. Remember one of my rules of thumb. If it's not meant to go into your body then simply don't put it in there.

My recommendation is to read this book four or more times a year for as long as it takes to rid yourself of your afflictions. Everything I have written, I lived through. The nine years I spent trying to free myself from my self created hell and the eight years I've been away from my old stomping grounds. That gives me seventeen years worth of working knowledge trying to beat my afflictions. Not to mention the time I spent on the streets watching others make failed attempts to free themselves from their afflictions. If you do everything that I suggest in this guide I believe you will win.

Many Worlds in One

What do I mean when I say many worlds in one? Each and every life that supports the human race is a world of its own. No one human being sees life in the same way. We are all different but yet very much the same. Life experiences for each of us are different. These differences create the world in which you exist. Your life or world is different than anyone else's. You and whom you believe in, create the world in which you choose to exist. Good, bad, or indifferent you exist in a much bigger world, which is planet earth itself.

Now let me go physics on you. Everything in existence is based on mathematics. The make up of our existence is based on a mathematical equation, which creates our world and the solar system. These mathematical equations create a balance that enables life in the galaxy to exist. All of this is accounted for in numbers.

Now what do you think your percentage is for abstaining from your abuse for any length of time? There is only a 16% chance in your favor of beating the odds. Against you is an 84% chance that you will repeat your previous mistakes. I found out something interesting. Faith the size of a mustard seed can change everything. Physics may explain how the universe was formed, but it can't explain why the success rate is so low after traditional treatment.

The things that seem impossible can be achieved. Scientists that believe in the same belief and objective will use mathematics, research, and experiments to amaze us every day. You see everything in our existence is based on mathematics and opposites. How does this all apply to you? You have to believe in that sixteen percent chance that you can succeed. As well in the possibility that you can overcome your current situation and live life to it's fullest, established because of a belief in yourself. Remember you are the creator of your own world. How do you want your self-chosen world to be?

Differences in Drug Treatments

Some abuses are accepted in our society and done openly with other people. But many abuses have to be kept in the closet because they are illegal. If you go to a bar to have a drink, no one says anything to you. They don't know if you abuse alcohol or not. But if you go to a bar and light up a crack pipe, you will probably be taking a trip to jail. So I believe there is a higher level of denial from people who have illegal abuses. These people are less likely to talk about these abuses for fear of being an outcast or going to jail.

Social drugs, such as alcohol and prescription drugs are harder to abstain from because they are legal until you abuse them. Meetings are the desired treatment for social abuses. In-house treatment centers are desired for non-social abuses. You have to separate yourself completely from your source of abuse.

When you go to meetings for non-social abuses you will at some point take a step backwards or abuse yourself again. You cannot treat these abuses socially because you are not able to sever yourself from your past. People's stories will constantly trigger you. Remember to leave your past behind you. You have to let go. Treatment for an infection is not the same as treatment for a broken bone. Different problems have different solutions.

Point of Interest

Now what do I mean by point of interest? A point of interest is nothing more than a pinpoint of which direction YOU choose to go. This all depends on your desired interest. Remember everyone's desired point of interest will be different, especially since we as humans are so much alike but in fact totally different. Now your first point of interest should be you wanting to have a prosperous life and a desire to stray away from substance abuse. What are the main building blocks of becoming a success at your desired interest?

➤ Acceptance

➤ Correction

➤ Redirection

These three things are crucial to incorporate into your life. These things are my own philosophies. Accept it, correct it, and then redirect it. Now I ask you? Do you have a problem with abuse of any kind? I used to believe that I had a substance abuse problem. Different professional people constantly were telling me that I had a substance abuse problem. This is a complete fallacy.

As I progressed along during the course of my transition, I learned a valuable lesson during my new transition. I found without understanding of a whole problem, no problem can be corrected. My point is to see things for how they really are. If you think that you have a substance abuse problem then you are totally mistaken, even if you abuse yourself twenty-four hours a day seven days a week. What if I were to tell you that you don't have a problem but a situation?

You cannot begin your transition until you accept that you have an unbearable situation that cause's you nothing but negative outcomes. No matter what your situation is, accept it, correct it, and then redirect yourself. All problems can be addressed by observing your situation.

Acceptance: In my past I simply accepted crack cocaine and meth into my life. Then the problems came that stemmed from me accepting it into my life. These were a heavy consumption of crack cocaine and the need for large amounts of money to support my habit. This took me down the path I used to support my drug habit lifestyle leading me to living a decadent lifestyle.

Correction: Once you have accepted that you have an affliction then you can correct your situation. Seize the moment and change your life by changing one thing, your situation. Then everything will change automatically. By accepting your situation it can be corrected and then redirected. If you are like me then you probably don't have just one problem but several. If you accept your situation you can then correct the problems allowing you to simply redirect your life.

Redirection: Redirection is the changing of your current negative path. This you can apply only after changing the one thing that is causing your life to be dysfunctional.

How can we correct the problems at hand?

1. We have to determine which one of these problems are the worst.

2. What are the causes that determine we have a problem in the first place?

3. Look at the causes behind your problem.

4. Your solution should then appear for which course of action you should be taking based on the causes that are complicating your existence. This is how you create a solution to your problems.

Example: I existed from day to day as I constantly smoked crack. I had many problems due to smoking crack on a daily basis. I looked at the causes that made my existence miserable. The main problem that appeared was my situation from smoking crack in the first place. The observations I made were my inability to hold a job, be in a relationship, maintain a dwelling and keep control over my actions. The causes behind my afflictions stemmed from my desire to escape reality. My revealed solution was leaving that miserable environment PERIOD!

The results are I'm a true survivor, which allows me to live a life with promise. I can honestly say that the problems in my life now are different then when I abused myself with crack. Most of my previous problems disappeared the moment that I changed my old situation. I now have a brand new set of unfamiliar problems. I have learned to create solutions to the situations in which caused me problems. I accepted the terms and then was able to correct my problems by a situation change.

I hope I'm getting you to see what I've seen. My point is to acknowledge that you are faced with a situation not one problem. Accept your situation, correct it, and then redirect your current path. Understanding of this should change your perception of things. I determined this through many trials and errors.

After accepting that I wasn't faced with one problem but a situation, I allowed for the healing process to begin. Do you see how changing one point can change the way you see one thing, which can change the outcome of everything. Including the way you see things now. This is one way you can create a changed destiny.

Overcoming Mood Swings and Anxiety Naturally

Each of us as human beings is gifted with the resilience of our bodies. Every human being has two sets of ears. One set of ears is attached to the outer part of our head. The other set is in the inner part of our head. Your outer ears hear the sounds of the physical world around you. Your inner ears hear the sounds your mind speaks telepathically.

The exercise you're going to apply is simply talking to yourself telepathically. Whenever an anxiety emerges you simply talk to yourself. Talk yourself out of your current anxiety. You will find in time that you can overcome your anxiety? Remember what I wrote earlier? "What you tell yourself makes all the difference." This is the exercise you will do to make that difference.

Example: When anxiety emerges simply talk to your self internally. Listen to what your mind is saying without reacting. After listening to your inner voice, think of all the situations you could be caught up in due to your anxieties. You can stay totally negative, but if you talk yourself out of feeding your anxiety then the anxiety will starve to death.

I learned this over time, but not before I lost myself several times in my anxieties. I learned how to abstain from abrupt anxieties by simply talking myself out of feeding into them in the first place. What happened for me then? I got past the anxieties that I experienced. I learned how to deal with new anxieties that came with the changes of life along with my behavior on a moments notice.

Marijuana

In this guide, I've written what worked for me. Now, these next writings might seem controversial, but anything else would in fact be a lie. After returning from my last slip back into my past existence I tried smoking marijuana. Why, you're wondering? That's just another abuse, you are thinking. Well, I smoked marijuana as a treatment for handling compulsive anxieties due to a bunch of unidentified negative emotions.

I can't tell you that I recommend you smoke marijuana because marijuana is illegal. I can tell you that in my new life marijuana worked to calm me down and allow me to think things through before making a mistake by returning to my past afflictions. Marijuana became one of the balances that I applied in my new life to alleviate anxiety and sudden mood swings. Don't get me wrong. I didn't use marijuana as an escape drug, but only as a treatment for unexpected high anxieties. It helped me to cope with the abrupt changes from negative to positive. I don't believe in prescription medicine or anxiety meds. I had been on those before and found you can abuse those just as easily as crack. I didn't want any more manmade chemicals being put into play in my life, and more importantly into my body. I used what God or Nature had available.

If you use prescription drugs to handle your unexplained anxieties, then a tragedy could most certainly occur. Ingesting too many manmade chemicals can cause you to overdose and die. I think we have seen this effect recently in the deaths of several famous people over recent years. Death is far worse than any anxiety attack.

I will back up my claim with my success. For me a couple of tokes off a joint when I was overstressed were better than going back to my crack affliction. Unless you've had a crack pipe in your mouth for a long period of time, you don't have any say. Unless you have firsthand experience of what an ex-crack or meth user goes through, you won't have a clue what I'm speaking about. It is hard to understand what a crack user goes through mentally and physically when quitting the abuse.

Again, I have five-plus years of no crack use after using crack for twenty-three years straight. Most importantly I have no more horrors in my life, and I don't have any more intolerable anxieties due to my past street life. I can honestly say that I now have total sobriety and am going strong.

If marijuana is legal in your state I strongly recommend it as a part of your treatment for the first several years of your new life to fight anxieties. Unfortunately, all drugs are political in some kind of way. Doctors should prescribe marijuana to crack and meth users as an anxiety suppressant. It does work. I'm sorry if this bothers some of my readers. But it is what it is. I care about helping people who are abusing themselves because I once abused myself in many different ways for long periods of time. I missed a lot of my life, and I don't want others to go through what I went through.

This guide is to help you see what I have seen

and what worked for me. Only you know which balances will work for you and only you. Please understand that if I didn't write about my use then this whole guide would be nothing short of a lie. I'd rather deal with controversy for the truth than be called out for a lie. At least you can say without a doubt that I'm honest, and I believe in this guide one hundred percent. Everything that I have written here has truthfully worked for me.

Marijuana helped me to get past compulsive anxiety disorders. I used marijuana only when I couldn't cope with the fear of life changing experiences. These anxiety attacks would occur about once a week in the beginning. These anxieties would send me backwards with a self-destructive mindset. I began creating arguments with my wife just to justify an excuse to run back to Tampa FL. Only so I could abuse myself conscience free. At first I kept repeating my past abuses at random.

After relapsing four times in two years I decided to do something different. The next time I started to experience a negative mood swing I decided to try smoking some marijuana. I quickly realized that this allowed me to calm down and re-evaluate my negative mindset. My abrupt mood swings grew farther and farther apart as more time passed. I can truthfully say that I haven't had a crack pipe in my mouth since March of 2005.

I will never forget how I once lived and won't go back to that existence. I can proudly say that I make my own choices and act freely of my own will. Ask yourself this, "If there were a drug that could help you to overcome anxiety would you take it?" I am sure you are saying yes without a doubt. Why? Because anything is better than the insane way you used to abuse yourself.

I found a revelation about myself. The first drug that I used which propelled me into insanity was in fact marijuana. I decided to use the same drug to get me out of insanity. It worked.

I came to this conclusion about drugs after using them for twenty-three years. Drugs don't lead you to other drugs. You lead yourself to other drugs by associating with people who do those drugs. By associating with these people you open yourself up to being nothing more then a human target. You support these other people by using these drugs with them.

Example: People who do crack cocaine, meth, opiates, or heroin usually will target marijuana smokers. They will simply become your friend and freely offer you other drugs out of pure projected glamour, as well as their desperate mindset to justify their usage. This brand new experience will seem so glamorous to you that the new drug will become more fulfilling than the marijuana.

You end up in your own self-created hell due to a single experience. The affliction at hand is what you're trading your soul for in the first place. This self-created hell is you being caught up in a decadent existence along with a bunch of rules and losers who will sweat you endlessly, especially if you feed them hard drugs. You'll create a miserable and lonely existence for yourself.

If you smoke marijuana then you should be on the look out for those people who abuse hard drugs. Disassociate yourself with them if you have any good sense at all. These people are losers by choice and action. No Exceptions!

People who abuse themselves with drugs should consider talking to a professional counselor or any counselor that deals with mental health issues on a regular basis. I recommend that you talk to someone before you considering using marijuana as a form of treatment.

Marijuana sometimes can create a depressed mindset depending on the person or where their abuse has led them up to the current moment mentally. Constant support from the winner or winners you feel the most comfortable with and applying all the contents in my guide will help you find your way.

I took my own advice and used marijuana as a part of my anxiety suppressant. It worked for me. I can deal with new life experiences and abrupt compulsive anxiety disorders up to the current moment when these anxieties occur. I don't use marijuana at this moment. I have learned how to deal with negative unidentified emotions without the use of anything chemically altering. But I must say. If I couldn't get through a life-changing event, I wouldn't hesitate to take a couple of tokes off a joint if it kept me from returning to my past existence of being a crack and meth junkie. Not to mention my other afflictions.

The world I have created for myself is

priceless compared to existing in the land of the walking dead. I escaped from the land of the walking dead for a purpose I believe; I have to spread this message. No matter what you've done to yourself during your past abuses, you can create a new world for yourself. A fulfilling world that is positive, where only the greatest of things exist.

My Recommended Drug Treatment Facilities

- Operation Par in Pinellas County, Florida
- The Salvation Army ARCs all across America
- DACCO of Hillsbourgh County, Florida
- Narconon all across America
- Acts Detox of Tampa, Florida
- Any place that deals with your type of chosen self-abuse

You can go to any drug treatment center that is nearest to you. Try any place that is close to your new location. Last but not least, try homeless shelters. Jails are also safe places where you're not likely to abuse yourself, but nobody wants to be there. If you're getting high and you need immediate help, do what you don't want to do and flag down a police officer. They can and usually will help you to get in one of these places. I totally recommend any residential drug treatment facility, as I myself have been in a few. Why? Because these facilities will separate you from the abuse while you learn tools that you will apply at some point after your release.

Now, when you where young and a mere child, your parents, teachers, or anyone who cared about you asked, "What do you want to be when you grow up?" Does this question sound familiar to you? Well, think about it. What was the answer to that question? Did you say a police officer, a fireman, or a pro football player? What did you say? I can pretty much guarantee that children who are asked that don't answer that they want to be a loser. If you didn't answer the question that you wanted to be a loser, then why would you want that for your life now? You see, what you tell yourself in each and every new moment will create the label you will become. This WILL affect the moment that you're in now as well as having a crucial impact on what your future will become.

Do you understand what I'm saying? Don't label yourself now as a loser; you didn't when you were a child. Guess what? You're a child again. You have to keep things simple and positive. If you do this, then you will be more successful. For example, when you go to meetings for any kind of abuse, you should address yourself by your given name only. Don't put the name of your abuse as a last name. You will live out who you tell yourself you are. That's why it is so important for you not to address yourself as a loser. I promise that your transition to your new life will be less complicated.

I want all the people who attend substance abuse meetings to know that I'm not knocking your meetings. I also attended lots of meetings throughout the time I attempted to have a better life. Most of the meetings were great and helped me considerably. But the truth is that I labeled myself in the beginning, addressing myself as "Rick, an addict." This made "me, myself, and I" totally believe that I was an addict. I really believed that I was helping myself by going to meetings as well as believing that I was an addict. This caused great confusion deep within me. How could I be a positive person if I were calling myself a negative? This kept me in a frame of mind that made me powerless and lacking the belief in my ability to overcome my afflictions.

Vitamins and Massages

As you are reclaiming your new life, I highly recommend vitamins. You have abused your body and most likely depleted many vitamins due to your affliction. I recommend Nature's Best vitamins as they are a good quality and can be obtained at any drug store.

The vitamins below are just some of what you will need to replenish your body if you can afford them. If not, you're not getting off that easy. Just take a good multi-vitamin to help you as much as possible. I took these vitamins myself, and I could actually feel my strength come back two months after taking them. Vitamin and mineral supplements are an important part of your life for better health.

Niacin No-Flush– To rid your body of the toxins from your cells. At first you will need a larger dose.

Multi-B Vitamins – To help with nerve repair and the stress of your new life.

Fish Oils – To strengthen your immune system, increase brainpower, and lubricate your joints.

Zinc, Selenium, and Magnesium – To help your body regulate sugar and healing.

Vitamin E – To repair cell damage.
Calcium – To strengthen bones.

Vitamin D – Many people have been found to be deficient in this vitamin, which is needed for your body to absorb Calcium properly.

Massages are also great for relieving tension and will help to keep your anxieties to a minimum. A good combination for massage oil is almond oil with lavender. Lavender is great for relieving stress and relaxing. When having a back massage, make sure the person uses a clockwise circular motion to move with your own natural energy flow.

Authors Points

Understanding Credibility

Once you take action, don't expect people you left behind to give you praise or credibility for your success. Why? Because the people you left behind can only see you as you were or who you used to be, not who you have become. Usually, these people you left behind, such as ex-husbands, ex-wives, other family, and acquaintances, will be negative. It's only because they can't accept the truth of who you have become in this moment. You don't owe these past people anything. You only owe yourself. These are your accomplishments, achieved goals, and dreams. You're never going to be a hero where you previously lived, because you left behind your past where all negative occurrences existed, including your past self.

Obtaining Hobbies

What is a hobby? A hobby is nothing more than an extra balance that is your personal passion or desire you adopt into your current life. Hobbies are great because of the expression of your inner self. Hobbies are also great for teaching you how to get through your extra time in a positive way. They are great for teaching you things or passions about yourself. You will find out what you can accomplish as well as gain a sense of determination to succeed. You can't go wrong if you introduce hobbies into your current life. Why? Because having too much time on your hands is never good. You see, idle time is the devil's playground. I'm sure you have heard that phrase. Believe me, it's true.

Change Itself

By changing one thing everything else will automatically change. The first thing that you will have to change is your death and destructive mindset. Secondly you will have to change your desire for resistance. Third you will have to change a negative attitude. At the beginning of your new life you will have to change all three things in order to move forward. You are the only one that can take action and do this. Control your actions and you'll be able to control yourself.

The Similarities of Trees and Human Beings

Trees and human beings are similar in many ways. One way is that we are all connected to part of the earth itself. Another way is that we both produce young. What if I was to tell you that you, as well as a tree, could disburse seeds?

You have these particular seeds inside of you already. These seeds are deep in your mind waiting for you to plant them. I call these particular seeds the seeds of new life. Once you plant these seeds a whole new life will develop deep inside of yourself. Nurturing this newly planted seed will create a strong tree over time. You will become that strong tree. This particular seed is your new beginning.

Self-Incorporation

What do I mean by self-incorporation? Self-incorporation is nothing more than the below list of eleven things that you will incorporate into your newly desired life. You will need to incorporate these things into your whole being.

1. Acceptance

2. Respect

3. Admiration

4. Appreciation

5. Comfortableness

6. Fun

7. Non-exclusion

8. Honesty

9. Patience

10. Commitment

11. Discipline

Once you have incorporated these eleven things into your life, you can then incorporate them into your relationships with others. It is very important to incorporate these eleven things into yourself as well as into your relationships with others. ONCE INCORPORATED INTO YOUR LIFE, THEY WILL HAVE A STRONG POSITIVE EFFECT ON ALL OF YOUR RELATIONSHIPS THROUGHOUT YOUR LIFE!

In other words treat people how you would want to be treated. I call this self-incorporation, a new incorporation of self. Remember all human beings require these eleven things to have fully functional healthy relationships with other people from all walks of life.

Closing Comment

Well, I have shared with you everything that I have done myself. I have been successful in staying off crack and meth after twenty-three years. I applied all of what I've written in this guide to my life and have been off crack for five years, going on six. The big thing for me is that I don't have the desire anymore. I believe that is because I do not associate with anyone from my past, and I only hang around winners. Remember, life will throw you a lot of curve balls, and how you handle them makes all the difference.

The Beginning